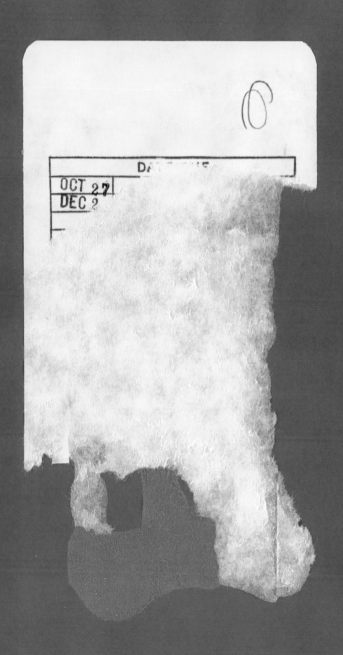

DA_____

OCT 27
DEC 2

First Things First

AN ILLUSTRATED COLLECTION OF SAYINGS
‹ USEFUL AND FAMILIAR FOR CHILDREN ›

BETTY FRASER

HARPER & ROW, PUBLISHERS

First Things First
Copyright © 1990 by Betty Fraser

Library of Congress Cataloging-in-Publication Data
Fraser, Betty.
    First things first.

    Summary: An illustrated collection of familiar
proverbs with suggestions for their proper use.
    1. Proverbs, American.   2. Proverbs, English.
[1. Proverbs]   I. Title.
PN6429.F73   1990   398'.921   86-42993
ISBN 0-06-021854-1
ISBN 0-06-021855-X (lib. bdg.)

Designed by Andrew Rhodes

1 2 3 4 5 6 7 8 9 10

First Edition

First Things First

AN ILLUSTRATED COLLECTION OF SAYINGS
❮ USEFUL AND FAMILIAR FOR CHILDREN ❯

What to say when you are the first

What to say when you are the last

What to say when you are tired of hearing someone talk about it

What to say when everyone is bossy and nothing gets done right

Too many cooks spoil the broth

What to say when everyone helps

Many hands make light work

What to say when you find something you would like to keep

Honesty is the best policy

What to say
when you can't do it the first time

If at first you don't succeed, try, try again

What to say
when you see people doing the same things

Birds of a feather
flock together

What to say
when you had to find out for yourself

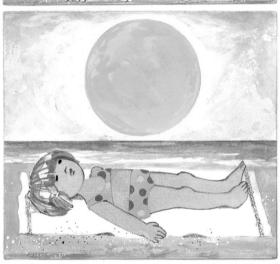 

Experience
is the best teacher

What to do when you don't know what to say

What to say when it seems as though what someone else has is better

What to say when things go badly

Into each life some rain must fall

Misery loves company

After Clouds Sunshine

Every cloud has a silver lining

What to say when you didn't believe it

Seeing is believing

Seeing is believing

Seeing is believing

Seeing is believing

Seeing is believing

Seeing is believing

What to say
when it isn't what you thought it would be

Things are seldom
what they seem

What to say when you need help

What to say when you pay someone back

One good turn deserves another

What to say
when you feel brave and ready to do it

Don't put off till tomorrow
what you can do today

Don't put off till tomorrow
what you can do today

What to say
when you aren't ready

What to say when someone is going too fast

What to say when someone is going too slow

What to say
when you spill it, drop it, or break it

What to do when you don't know what to do

Do unto others as you would have them do unto you

What to say when it's all done

All good things must come to an end